THE HEALING POWER OF GRATITUDE

A COMPLETE GUIDE TO HEALING DEPRESSION AND ANXIETY WITH GRATITUDE

PORTIA CRUISE

© 2019 Portia Cruise

All rights reserved.

You are welcome to join the Fan's Corner, here

Disclaimer

The advice and strategies found within may not be suitable for every situation. This work is sold with the understanding that neither the author nor the publisher is held responsible for the results accrued from the advice in this book.

Chapter 1

Introduction

A lot of people associate anxiety with mental health challenges, yet without anxiety, the inbuilt human mechanism for reacting to situations that demands our immediate reaction would be lost.

Anxiety is what helps us respond properly to perceived danger or a situation that has the potential of leading to unwanted consequences. It is anxiety that helps analyze a scenario so that we are able to decide if we should stay and fight or if we should adopt flight as a better alternative. The anxiety you get before your next exam or interview is usually necessary because it allows you to tap into the positive aspect of anxiety and prepare adequately for the exam. It is that anxiety that will help you take adequate precautions to put the situation under control so that you find that you are far more able to manage the situation better than you would have if the anxiety was totally absent.

Another way to understand anxiety is to see it as what makes us react and stamp on the brakes when we notice a child run into the road as we drive on the highway, in this situation, the human instinct is heightened and more blood is pumped to the brain, which now has to make quick decisions to try and ensure there is no accident, so you see that anxiety is not such a bad thing.

However, anxiety as a disorder is a major cause of concern when the anxiety is sustained or occurs because of very trivial issues that should ordinarily not ignite it and when it occurs, it stays longer than is necessary. Anxiety can lead to chronic and excessive worrying, which can, in turn, lead to shortness of breath, fatigue, insomnia, and nausea.

That is not all, it can further escalate into increased risk of stroke, memory loss, and poor performance in the workplace or school. Persistent anxiety is a major area of concern because of the tendency for it to lead to social anxiety, panic disorder, or generalized anxiety disorder.

Anxiety disorder is common in the US, with nearly 40 million adults diagnosed as having the ailment. It also affects all genders, race or age group.

The standard treatment for anxiety used by practitioners is the use of psychotherapy, like Cognitive Behavioral Therapy (CBT). This is frequently combined with counseling or non-therapeutic ways of managing stress and anxiety. While there are various forms of Non-Therapeutic means of managing anxiety, the use of gratitude is beginning to get increased recognition as an effective self-help way of managing anxiety disorder.

Until recently, not many people saw the link between gratitude and anxiety, however, which is no longer the case for a lot of people. More and more people are beginning to notice significant improvements in their anxiety problems by focusing more on being grateful for even the smallest of things in life. As simple and easy as this may seem, it has been known to lead to a gradual change in mindset which can ultimately lead to a reduction in anxiety over time.

When you suffer from anxiety, it is hard to see how gratitude can be helpful to you, but living a life of gratitude and being grateful for the things of life can lead to a change in mindset and a significant improvement in your physical, mental and spiritual health.

Being Grateful as a Form of Gratitude

Gratitude helps you to be thankful, extend an appreciation and reciprocate kindness. It is a state of mind that we attain by acknowledging the positive things in our lives while appreciating those things we consider small. It also has to do with the ability to recognize and acknowledge the people, good things and places in our lives.

It is gratitude that makes a person thankful enough to show appreciation for the tangible or intangible things the individual has received, enabling them to acknowledge the goodness in their lives.

Gratitude is an emotion just like anxiety and can be described as a feeling that occurs at an interpersonal level, which allows a person to acknowledge and appreciate receiving a personal benefit that may or may not, have been intentionally sought after, deserved or earned.

Gratitude can be learned when it does not come naturally, which means virtually anybody can practice it. You can start by identifying the aspects of your life that require appreciation and knowing how best to show appreciation for them. Anxiety can make us trapped in our fears and thoughts, whereas gratitude can help remove us from such traps and instead help us focus on an interpersonal relationship with other people and the environment in which we live in.

Knowing what gratitude is, is one thing, but knowing what to do to show our gratitude is another, the following actions can help us towards living a life that is filled with gratitude.

1. Don't be picky about what you should be grateful for, appreciate everything around you. The habit of being grateful starts with appreciating everything in life and acknowledging that there is nothing too small to be thankful for.

2. Always find gratitude in your challenges, no matter what those challenges are.

3. Deliberately practice mindfulness, sit daily and think of things you can actually be grateful for.

4. Always learn to put down your positive thoughts in writing, this will help you focus your attention on the subject matter. You can journal your gratitude journey on a regular basis using the "Workbook for The Healing Effect of Gratitude".

5. Learn to always give back to others in the local community, this will help you to be more grateful and take fewer things for granted.

6. For gratitude to have its positive effects, it has to be expressed and not kept to oneself. The person, group or entity whose action is worthy of note and is deserving of our gratitude should not be kept in the dark but should be aware of our level of gratitude.

7. Spend time with loved ones.

8. While it is no brainer that the actions that cause us to be grateful tend to make us happy, expressing our gratitude to others also has the capacity to make us happy and our capacity to be

grateful is also significantly increased when we are already happy.

Gratitude is sometimes also known in some quarters as grace, acknowledgment, gracefulness, appreciative, praise, recognition, and responsiveness.

Unlike gratitude, anxiety is more than just feeling stressed or worried, it is how we respond to situations where we feel pressured.

Symptoms of Anxiety

When we feel a lot of stress, we can be affected negatively, which can result in a wide range of symptoms, including mood disorders, depression and even substance abuse by people who are not able to handle the feelings of anxiety or stress. This situation can further escalate to low self-esteem, panic attacks, inability to sleep, obsessive thoughts and disorientation. That is why when anxiety becomes consistent and stays for a long period of time after the threat or trigger has passed, then it may be classified as an anxiety disorder.

There are different categories of anxiety disorder, some of which include the following;

Generalized Anxiety Disorder

Those with this type of anxiety disorder have an exaggerated sense of worry over everything, including trivial things even if there is nothing that provokes it.

Obsessive-Compulsive Disorder (OCD)

Obsessive-Compulsive Disorder, OCD, is an anxiety disorder that is characterized by recurring, intrusive and unwanted thoughts that are classified as obsessive. These thoughts tend to be repeated which is why it is called compulsive. People with this disorder worry and fear the worse about anything and everything. Even when they acknowledge that their thoughts are silly, in a bid to get temporal relief, they still go ahead to indulge in repetitive behaviors that include checking already locked doors, washing hands consistently, and washing their clothes every time because they worry about germs.

Panic Disorder

This type of anxiety disorder is characterized by unpredictable, intense fear and an overwhelming feeling of anxiety followed by repeated episodes of shortness of breath, heart palpitations, dizziness, and chest pain. When a person suffers from recurrent panic attacks or consistent fears for a period that exceeds more than one month, they are said to suffer from panic disorder.

Post-Traumatic Stress Disorder (PTSD)

This type of anxiety disorder can develop after a person has been exposed to a traumatic experience or event in which serious physical injury may have occurred.

Some traumatic experiences that are capable of triggering PTSD include accidents, violent personal attack, combat events, wars, gun battle and other forms of disaster. This disorder is characterized by symptoms of the person's inability to relax, disturbing nightmares or flashbacks of the traumatic experience, and a desire to avoid anything that is related to the event.

The most common way of diagnosing PTSD is when a person has symptoms that last longer than one month.

Social Phobia (or Social Anxiety Disorder)

Humans as social animals tend to be conscious of how others perceive us, but those with social phobia or sometimes referred to as Social Anxiety Disorder have a far higher intense fear of being criticized, humiliated or scrutinized. For some people, it can be as mild as when the person has a fear of speaking in both formal and informal settings or can be in its most severe form where they experience anxiety disorder symptoms just being in the company of people.

Specific Phobia

Similar to social phobia is specific phobia. In this type of disorder, the person is unable to overcome the fear of doing a particular thing even though there is no need to fear and no matter the reassurances. Such fears may include phobia of heights, flying or water.

Chapter Two

Expressing Gratitude

Expressing gratitude or showing appreciation is critical to our everyday life when we express gratitude; we communicate with the other people in our lives and let them know what they mean to us. The simple and effective ways to express gratitude include the following:

1. Be generous with kind words

   The quickest and easiest way to express gratitude is to say thank you, especially to those who look or feel distressed, lonely, unappreciated, ill, fatigued, or anxious.

   Expressing words of gratitude is not just an act of good manners, but also the most appropriate thing to do when someone helps you. Saying kind words may not repay the good things someone does for you, but it certainly goes a long way in creating the right impression.

   There are so many kind words that can be said to people as a way of expressing gratitude, such words usually convey a strong message and propel people to do much more. Some kind words include:

   - I appreciate the things you have done for me
   - You have no idea how much this means to me
   - I wonder how I could have done this without you
   - I am indebted to you
   - I am blessed to have you as a friend

- I cannot think of anything more amazing than you since you came along
- Thank you so much for the things you do for me

Expressing gratitude with kind words and not only shows good manners, but a simple expression of gratitude can go a long way in relationships and communication with others.

2. Include others in your plan

When you include others in your plans, it lets them know that you are thinking about them and value their friendship, it is also an effortless way to express your gratitude. It also helps them achieve a purpose, which can make them feel appreciated and build their self-esteem and value to themselves or to the larger society.

The fact is, it is not always convenient to include people in your plans, but the rewards of doing it are great. For example, reaching out and making out time for a sick friend or relative could just be all you need to express gratitude to that person who has been of help in the past.

3. Offer to do errands, help with chores

People are often in need of someone to run errands for them and assist with their chore, which is why helping a colleague with their projects, or taking friends and family to the park or to relaxation centers all counts as a way of showing gratitude to them and to nature. A lot of people are stressed out today and helping them out can relieve them of their stress.

4. Deliver flowers or a bouquet to loved ones

Another amazing way you can show your gratitude is by giving a bouquet of flowers as a thank you gift. Such gifts are not always about the cost, but also the feelings attached to the action that shows how much you appreciate them. A flower is an amazing way to express gratitude to friends who deserve it.

5. Call to say hello

Gratitude can also be expressed by calling a deserving person just to say hello to the person without any string attached, calls tend to be gratifying to both caller and receiver, the exchange of pleasantries helps to build a rapport.

6. Pay impromptu visits

We all need people at different points in our lives, and so a surprise visit from someone special even if the visit is a quick one always has a positive effect. Such people will appreciate your visit especially when such persons have invited you over time. Paying an impromptu visit is a way of expressing gratitude and showing people that they are truly loved and appreciated. Nobody is an island.

7. Ask if there is anything that can be done

Not everyone is willing to ask for help even when they need it so you can learn to show gratitude to nature and people around you by finding out from them if there is anything you can do for them, such show of gratitude can help our loved ones know we appreciate them.

8. Email to check them up

If you are busy and can't take the time for a personal visit, you can always use the email to reach out to loved ones, you can write a carefully communicated note to let the person know he or she is in your thoughts.

9. Listen intently

    You can show gratitude to somebody who means a lot to you by showing up to lunch and listening up to whatever they want to say and resisting the urge to interrupt them.

10. Give a long intimate hug if you can or stick out your hand for a handshake depending on the preference of the person.

11. Compliment people for their respective talents, skill set, areas of strength which you admire in them.

12. Gratitude can be shown to a worker by providing techniques or ideas that make their workload easier to manage.

13. You can bring back lunch for an employee or colleague if you know they are working hard and haven't had time to get lunch.

14. Show gratitude to your boss by letting them know that they are doing a great job and contributing to the company.

15. Acknowledging something people are able to do well is one way we can show gratitude to people who serve you.

16. Appreciate friends for showing you new ways of addressing old issues, even if their point of view differs from their own.

17. Invite family members, including your aged parents to do something that has been their lifelong dream.

18. Volunteer to help others do things you know they don't like doing.

19. Be prepared to stay calm, controlled and collected even in a stressful situation.

20. Also, learn to appreciate yourself in whatever positive you think suitable.

Importance of Gratitude

Cultivating the habit of being grateful for every good thing that comes to you and gives thanks continuously can have a great impact on your life.

Most people associate gratitude with only saying thank you or showing appreciation to someone who has helped us or given us a gift, we should, however, take note from the scientific point of view that gratitude is not just an action but it is a positive emotion which is really important because it serves a purpose.

If you were ever in doubt about the importance of gratitude, below are some reasons why you should consider gratitude an important aspect of your life:

1. Acts of gratitude are helpful as a way to apologize, make amends or help solve problems other people may face.
2. People can use gratitude to form new social relations or to build upon and make the current relationships count.
3. Gratitude generally makes people admire us. It makes our overall attitude to be nicer, more trusting, and sociable, which helps us acquire more friends, deepen their already existing relationships and marriage.
4. Gratitude can boost our career-this means that gratitude makes people more effective managers, helps in networking, increases decision-making capabilities, increases productivity and helps in

getting more mentors and protégés. As a result of all these, gratitude can help achieve career goals, as well as make your workplace a more friendly and enjoyable place to be.

5. Gratitude increases the strength of our emotion, reduces feelings of envy, and enhances improvement in memory. Gratitude creates a sense of good feelings that has a direct impact on stress.

6. It makes us less self-centered, the very nature of gratitude is to focus on the acts of the benevolence of others, in this regard, gratitude practice can be better than therapy on self-esteem.

7. People with high energy levels tend to display the same qualities that most grateful people have.

8. Gratitude is not something that is meant to just give us a feeling of being good or just make people happier, it is happiness in itself. The act of showing gratitude makes both the person expressing it and the recipient happy.

9. Gratitude drives away envy and jealousy.

10. When you have gratitude, you are more likely to be friendlier with those around you. Gratitude tends to also be associated with kindness, which gets people to want to reciprocate.

11. Compared to ingratitude that is generally treated with contempt, gratitude is considered a virtue that attracts more positive gestures.

12. If we practice gratitude, we will never run short of admirers and friends who genuinely love us.

13. Gratitude will help you network and socialize better. Grateful people tend to be more likely to help others which help improve their network.

14. Grateful people beam with self-esteem and self-belief, which helps them improve their focus and productivity.

15. Grateful people are healthier people.

16. Gratitude can relieve the stress that a person feels.

17. Gratitude is also beneficial to couples and makes them have more positive feelings towards each other.

18. For anyone in the process of recovering from an injury, gratitude acts as an immune booster.

19. For those with sleeping related problems, it is observed that thinking of things to be grateful for can make them drift off to sleep.

Chapter Three

The Healing Power of Gratitude

A lot of people are stressed up, with more to do, with far less time to do it, making it a common occurrence to see a lot of persons struggling to strike a balance with respect to their career, time, finance, and family. These activities have to be combined with trying other important needs that include being in a good state of health and wellbeing. Fortunately, there are a lot of solutions that can be easily gotten.

The stress experienced by individuals come from different sources that span from the physical inactivity we undertake to the anxiety about the future, family members and relationships. Sometimes, it is in the form of pains on various part of the body, which serves to give some form of indications that there could be a problem in the body. The result of these can lead to the experience of certain forms of physical or mental condition that may or may not require medical attention. Some of these conditions end up resulting in other more serious ailments like cardiovascular disease, diabetic conditions, obesity, and cancer.

Stress is not just about what goes on in our life, but also about how those things are perceived. Luckily, although we cannot control what happens around us, we can, however, control our perception and understanding of these things.

Effects of Gratitude on Healing

For years, the only studies that were done on the relationship between emotions and physical health only had to do with negative emotions such as anger, fear, and hopelessness, it was not until recently that studies were also carried out on understanding the link between the positive aspects of our emotions and how they relate to our state of mind, mental health and well being.

Gratitude is a common theme in the wellness community and anyone with regular practice, no matter the health practice, gratitude will always come up since studies began to focus on the positive side of emotions. Feelings of gratitude can have a very big effect on the body and physical health. The end results of these studies show a clear connection between the cultivation of positive emotional states and healing from and surviving some major illnesses, cancer not excluded.

When we exhibit positive emotions, the stiffening bodily reactions and narrowing thoughts are greatly reduced, instead, there will be a broadening and expanding on all levels. The mind, therefore, opens to greater possibilities. The end result of this expansion includes changes in breathing patterns and pulse as well as balancing out of hormone levels and blood pressure. According to science, gratitude might just be the most important tool we need to maintain health and happiness all through the year.

Why people have Problems Expressing Gratitude

The most important factor in a long and happy life is having a good social network you can depend on, every day we cooperate with others, we help them and they help us too, yet in our daily activities, we often fail to express gratitude to those who make a difference in our lives.

Gratitude has never been known to come easy and is a diminishing virtue in modern times. Humans tend to focus on what they lack or on what other people have that they do not have, a lot of people have difficulty displaying their gratitude for one reason or the other and remain mute even when they know they should be expressing gratitude. Because of how our brains work, we tend to over-focus on painful and negative events while ignoring the pleasant experiences. The truth is that, the more we experience, the less we are naturally inclined to notice opportunities for gratitude.

Some of the reasons, why people refuse to express gratitude, are:

1. Struggle for the right words to use

People could be short of words when trying to express gratitude, the struggle of knowing what to say and how to say can hinder some people from expressing their gratitude to people who have shown them a kindness at one or the other. Some people even assume that the receiver will feel uncomfortable if they express gratitude to them.

2. They are uncomfortable

Some people have difficulty expressing their feelings, they find it difficult to put the right words together and opt instead to sometimes say nothing. Some others misinterpret certain kind gestures to be a form of inducement or as an action done to curry a favor in future and so do not see the need to be grateful.

3. They don't realize your effort

Some people underrate the effort of others and so do not bother to show gratitude to the person who has gone out of his way to having something done for them. Even the smallest labor deserves some acknowledgment.

4. Distractions

Some people are so occupied with other things and might not even remember to acknowledge the effort of another person, for instance, someone who has been working late nights or working very hard to meet up with a deadline might not remember to express gratitude as a result of the pressure of work. This could be an oversight on the part of the receiver which is not necessarily intentional.

5. Time and habit

Our daily habits develop from what it takes us from one moment to the next, daily routines from our everyday habits and due to all these people might just forget to appreciate the kind gestures that are shown on a daily basis, for instance, the mailman who drops the mail every week might not get much gratitude compared to the courier that comes with a package at long intervals. Also, time and habits might reduce the rate at which people express gratitude to the folks around them.

6. When you are actually ungrateful

Some people actually don't express gratitude because of the entitlement mentality, they feel entitled to the kind gesture of others and so do not see the need to show gratitude to such people, such people are simply ungrateful and expressing gratitude to others is not something they deem fit.

7. There is unresolved conflict

Whenever there is a sense of hostility from one person to another, there is less chance of being able to communicate in a positive manner. Especially when the issues have not been resolved, one party will refuse to acknowledge the other person action and deny them the gratitude so that they do not assume that their action has been forgiven and forgotten. The person is therefore deemed not qualified to enjoy the general niceties that other less contending folks may be receiving. The fact is that not showing appreciation to someone who has been kind enough to do something nice to us despite their previous grievance adds to the existing discords and sends the message of indifference which can strain both social and workplace relationships.

8. You have become complacent

This kind of person is satisfied with whatever life has thrown at him and so do not see any need to be particularly grateful.

Cultivating the Healing Power of Gratitude

Gratitude is a powerful tool that helps us expand our lives, create loving relationships, and even improve our health. Cultivating gratitude takes practice, the more we do it, the better we get at it and the better we start to feel and this is something we can actually work towards, in other words, it is possible to cultivate gratitude.

Leaning to focus on gratitude has the effect of improving the overall emotional wellbeing, physical health, and mental state.

A life of gratitude is more likely to provide you with happiness, joy, energy and a fullness of heart that moves us from limitation and fear of expansion and love. Gratitude brings our attention into the present, which is the only where miracles can unfold, the deeper our appreciation, the more we see with the eyes of the soul and the more our life flows in harmony with the creative power of the universe.

To benefit from the healing power of gratitude, here are a few powerful gratitude practices for you to try:

1. Keep a gratitude journal

Cultivating gratitude as an attitude is a key component of experiencing high levels of being happy, fulfilled, and general well being. This attitude helps to achieve a higher purpose in life and increases the number of joyful moments in our lives. The best way to keep a gratitude journal is to challenge yourself to ensure each event is unique, which will in turn force you to think deeply to appreciate even those things you consider trivial even though they are capable of enhancing your life.

To ensure consistency, you may decide to fill the journal moments before you go to bed or as you wake up in the morning, or just before you meditate. The time isn't as important as the fact that you take a few moments to focus your mind on your blessings. This job of the gratitude journal is to help you appreciate life a lot more.

2. Write a thank you letter

This activity is a very important one because it entails generating a list of people who have made a tremendous impact on your life, you can decide a write a letter of thanks expressing your gratitude to such persons, where possible you can deliver your letter of gratitude in person. Although it is more common to thank people verbally, a written form of gratitude can be equally effective. A letter can be re-read and treasured, creating joy and love that will continue to ripple out into the universe.

3. Take a gratitude walk

When you are feeling down or stressed down, you can take a gratitude walk for about twenty minutes around your area, in a park, around your office, or anywhere with open space. Walking affords you the opportunity to reflect on the things you are grateful for, nurture relationships, helps you to burn some of your unwanted fats. You can also use the opportunity of your gratitude work to be grateful for the air you breathe which makes your life possible. When used properly, gratitude walk becomes a powerful tool in shifting your mood to open you to the flow of abundance that surrounds you.

4. Volunteer

You can take advantage of the enormous opportunities in volunteering at churches, local shelters, and wherever help is required to exercise your level of gratitude. The benefits of also giving your time to others are enormous, apart from the contact and the people you meet, there is also the universal law of nature that ensures you are rewarded in some way or the other.

5. Go to therapy

When the daily struggles your life clogged up your mind, the tendency to have difficulty appreciating the value of gratitude in your life increases. In such situations, you may need to talk to the therapist who is trained to deal with such issues. Our mental health determines to a large extent our ability to interpret and analyze events happening around us.

6. If you are faith driven, cultivate it

If you are a religious person and believe in the concept of faith, then you will find gratitude to be one of your most potent weapons to feel it. Your act of gratitude to your creator will act to further inspire you to have faith in the belief that whatever you have asked for will be given to you in due time. This is a universal law and is independent of the faith you practice.

7. Take time to reflect

It is easy to allow frustration and disappointments have a negative influence over your life when all you think about are the negative thoughts that fight for prominence in our lives. But if we are able to take some moments off and reflect on the various aspects of our lives, we will be able to find reasons why we should have gratitude in your life. When we reflect on gratitude, we discover as others have done before, it's power as a tool that helps us expand our lives, create loving relationships, and even improve our health. However, cultivating gratitude requires constant practice and it gets easier as we get better at doing it.

8. Set a Fixed Time for Positive Gratitude Affirmations

To start getting used to sending out positive affirmations of gratitude, it may be important to have a specific time of the day to remind yourself of the things you need to be grateful for. A lot of people have found this to be an effective way of connecting with gratitude during the day, even during your busy schedule at work, regular activities, attending to kids, or being at home.

The simple act of scheduling this kind of activity ahead of time, helps sends a positive signal to the brain to constantly be on the lookout for positive situations or moments so that you are able to do that exercise properly, that can help you begin to notice more of positive events than the negative ones that had hitherto been the focus of your attention.

Chapter Four

Using Natural Methods with Gratitude to Reduce Anxiety

The link between gratitude and anxiety is quite astonishing and in many being grateful for things no matter how simple they are can help in relieving anxiety as a whole. This is because when you have gratitude, you see the good in every situation which enables you to see the light no matter how dark the moment is.

It is very likely that a person with anxiety disorders will have his head full of mental burden, such a person will always be filled with anxious thinking, isolation and all manner of things that come with anxiety. Expressing gratitude isn't a magic wand that will drive away from the anxiety and being appreciative or showing gratitude doesn't mean you have to be grateful for having anxiety but it can rewrite your brain to experience less anxiety.

How Gratitude can be used to Drive Anxiety Away

It can seem difficult to imagine that gratitude can help in relieving or reducing anxiety, especially when you are struggling to find things to be grateful for.

Anxiety overburdens the brain and causes a lot of distress to the brain, anxiety can feel like a thick fog has surrounded the mind, nothing feels really enjoyable and it makes the world look hazy-hopeless. The anxious thought acts as a barrier to experiencing the world and this feeling of separation can lead one to feel even more upset as it can even lead to fear of losing oneself. Studies have shown that expressing gratitude helps to reduce anxiety, especially when you are well rested. When you feel stressed or brain fog, just put gratitude into full practice and you will definitely feel better.

A lot has already been said about the arts of gratitude and the benefits it can bring, gratitude can have such a powerful impact on your life because it engages your brain in a virtuous cycle, your brain only has so much power to focus its attention, it can only easily focus on one thing at a time, either positive or negative stimuli, you can't be grateful and anxious at the same time, anxiety has less power within the grateful mind. Gratitude can go a long way in reducing your anxiety disorders by concentrating less on the load on the head and concentrating on the heart where gratitude can be developed. You can achieve this by closing your eyes and moving your attention to your heart area, after doing this, begin to concentrate on some things in your life that you can genuinely feel a deep appreciation for, there are so many things that one can show appreciation for, ranging from family to career, to business, to friends, to neighbors home, colleagues and so many good things of life. Gratitude is easy to ignore when you have anxiety disorder because we tend to focus on only the negative things around us during such moments. Gratitude goes beyond just having good manners, but a form of consciousness connected to your feelings and requires constant practice.

When you are suffering from anxiety, it can be very difficult to find things to show gratitude for, but the constant practice of daily gratitude can significantly contribute to shifts in your health both mentally and physically. Suffering from anxiety can be a very difficult thing and it is helpful to feel pity for yourself for going through such struggles and it can slow down and realize that on some levels a lot of things are to be appreciated in life.

An interesting thing about gratitude is that it is not something that our nature accepts easily, so even when you find it difficult to appreciate, just know that it is not far from your innate nature. We can, however, make a conscious effort to connect with the appreciation gene within us. A sufferer of anxiety can find it so hard to find joy, but gratitude helps distract you from anxious thoughts so you can see beyond the anxiety and connect to the present moment. When gratitude starts as a practice, it can gradually become more natural, when you are in the present moment, you have more reasons to be joyful and a lot fewer reasons to be anxious about. Rediscovering or making a great effort towards showing gratitude can shift your view of how you see yourself and the world. When anxiety makes you feel heavy, gratitude can make you feel light. We feel less of a need to control the future if only we can learn to appreciate the present, this can allow for easy relaxation.

Appreciating the positive aspects of life can change the activities of our brain, this can help enforce and help to build healthy habits, thus as you practice gratitude and it feels good, you will now start doing it on a continuous basis. A good night's rest gives our brains time to let go and reset for the next day and it has been proven over time gratitude leads to better sleep, people who experienced more gratitude fell asleep faster and sleep for a longer period than people who did not experience gratitude. Healthy sleep is fundamental for mental and physical well being and helps to reduce anxiety.

The practice of gratitude forces people suffering from anxiety to start thinking about other people and the way they contribute to their lives, when you start expressing gratitude, you will have less time to wallow and gaze at space and more time to notice how many kindnesses were shown regularly. Gratitude practice drastically reduces stress levels, there is even a lot of data to back this up, there is no chemical to make you happy but gratitude can help anyone achieve happiness. When you make a deliberate effort to be grateful all the time, the brain will begin to think positively, it is more natural to default to a positive take on things that happened.

The best way to overcome anxiety with gratitude is to simply decide each day to look for the good in my life and express gratitude for it, this means can become filled with a good if only we can express genuine gratitude all the time.

The more a sufferer of anxiety looks for good things in his life and in people around him, the more the brain becomes alert to good things, scans for good things and finds good things. When there is so much good around, there are fewer tendencies to be depressed, the brain naturally scans for bad and it is exceptionally good at finding it. Once it is realized that the thought can play a part in depression, a conscious effort should be made to replay certain things that one can be grateful for.

When we give thanks, we automatically focus our attention on what is working in our lives, instead of what is not working, this shift in perception can actually change brain chemistry and counter the negative thinking that depression is known for. You can begin each day by asking what is beneficial in your life right now, what you can be grateful for and who are working to support you in your health and healing, as you pay more attention to the good in your you will notice more and more of that good and through more of that attraction, you will attract more good to yourself because whatever you focus on expands.

Expressing gratitude does not mean you are not in pain or darkness, neither does it mean that you are denying the pain or uncomfortable feelings, but it helps you to recognize those points of lights that exist in the dark.

The victim of anxiety usually develops a victim mentality, which is always acting like the victim in all circumstances, the earlier we all realize that bad stuff happens to everyone and it is your choice to let yourself play the victim, the better for us all. Gratitude teaches you how to be empathic and helps you stop making yourself the center of attraction to people around you, the world doesn't revolve around anybody, it also helps you to catch a glimpse of how draining the misery can be on everyone, a depressed person does not emit joy to those around him or her.

Gratitude has an instantly rewarding practice that gives positive emotions that transition to a place where you are emotionally stronger and able to be emotionally self-controlled. Gratitude is a powerful antidote to depression. Feeling grateful brings emotions of awe, wonder, happiness, and joy, and these emotions shove aside depression in people.

Random acts of kindness can also kill depression, if all else fails and you feel you are getting depressed, just go out and do some secret acts of kindness for strangers and friends, it works like magic. Truth be told, there is something magical and soothing about rendering little acts of kindness here and there. Depression is no fun and it can be mentally draining and a lot of bad incidences have been associated with depression and anxiety, but trying out gratitude can help in alleviating depression and anxiety.

Sufferers of anxiety should always learn to laugh because it is hard to feel anxious when you are laughing, it is good for your health and also help in many ways to relieve stress and anxiety, laugher also helps in the long term to improve your immune system and mood. When stressed, anxious or depressed, try watching a funny video with friends and family.

Another key is to focus on being aware of smaller things in life and show gratitude for those little things of life, just imagine that you would miss those things if you are no longer on the earth, this is a very powerful practice that has been utilized by people from all walks of life, it means appreciating the little things of life to reduce anxiety.

A daily practice of gratitude can reduce anxiety and depression. One way to achieve this is by focusing your gratitude on some key areas, for example, write one thing about something you are grateful for every morning, which could be your finance, your career, your health, etc. It could also help to change the point of focus every other day. You can also show gratitude for the wind blowing on your face, the warmth of the coffee mug, the silence of your bedroom, running water, heat, the ability to run, the ability, to walk, the ability to eat, the ability to talk, the numerous friends you have and all other pleasures of life.

Children should also be encouraged to practice gratitude because children could also be victims of anxiety, so when gratitude is inculcated in children at an early age, it becomes easy for them to practice it as they grow older, gratitude reduces anxiety in children and this, in turn, helps them to get more sleep and even build stronger relationships. Children should be taught from an early age how to say thank you, gratitude doesn't come easy for children, so a deliberate effort has to be made for the young ones to grab the act of gratitude which actually goes beyond words and actions. Children should be encouraged at all times and at a very tender age to learn how to show gratitude even before they understand the real concept of gratitude. Teaching children how to be grateful comes with a lot of benefits which go beyond just being polite.

Good and healthy relationships can serve as buffers against being depressed or anxious which can lead to an improved form or life or aid in our recovery. So you can make your burden of anxiety lighter by expressing gratitude for any little thing that comes your way and for every kind gesture shown to you, including those very little things that you might think do not matter.

True gratitude can help you live a better life in spite of the person's anxiety, it doesn't completely remove anxiety but it reduces it. When you focus on how you view yourself and the world, it can help change your focus from what is wrong to what is right and this can have an adverse effect on the state of mind of the individual. While it is true that gratitude is not a magic wand that can cause the immediate disappearance of anxiety, it can, however, help build a new mindset that will help in ensuring that the anxiety gets reduced as time goes on. When you develop gratitude as a habit, it becomes also able to change your whole way of life to make you happier and healthier.

Practicing daily gratitude can contribute significantly to your mental and physical health. Expressing gratitude in your everyday life shouldn't be seen as a chore, as something that should be done under compulsion, it shouldn't be taken as a task; gratitude should be taken as a gentle approach to anxiety.

Gratitude allows you to be optimistic and being optimistic plays a major role in overcoming anxiety, after all when you are constantly seeing the negative sides of things, it can be hard to crawl out of the dark hole of negativity. Since gratitude rewires your brain to see the good aspect of things and of life, automatically you will now have a positive approach to life which will, in turn, reduce the stress of anxiety.

It also allows you to see past your anxiety, practice of gratitude can help you to see beyond your past and what is making you anxious, so you may be anxious about going to a social event, but with the new practice of gratitude, you will pay more attention to the fact that you get to see people you have missed. The good part is that it happens naturally, the positive thoughts fill up most part of your brain.

Ways to Naturally Reduce Anxiety

Since anxiety is a normal aspect of life, it is important not to perceive it as something that is so bad in itself, because it plays a very important role in making us aware and preparing for perceived dangers ahead, motivates us to stay organized, better prepared and propels us to acquire the right skills needed to deal with different situations, deadlines, projects and challenges. However, when anxiety becomes a regular daily struggle, and if left unchecked, it can greatly impact your quality of life negatively. When it gets to this level, it becomes important to take adequate steps to roll back the condition.

The knowledge that anxiety is a normal aspect of our life should convince all sufferers of anxiety to learn to always take a positive approach to life. By approaching life with a clearly defined purpose, it becomes easier to see anxiety as something not so evil that should be treated with a high level of contempt or fear.

As a long term solution to the treatment of anxiety, a sufferer should focus more on the use of easy, natural therapies that can be incorporated into everyday life, less intrusive and highly effective. The majorities of these methods are able to not only solve anxiety-related problems but are also very useful in the general well being of the individual. Things like early morning meditation, walking around the neighborhood, can go a long way in relieving one's self of stress and anxiety.

Managing Anxiety with Yoga

By living a life of gratitude and combining it with regular yoga practice, the symptoms of anxiety can be effectively managed.

As a regular exercise, yoga will be of benefits to both the physical and emotional aspects of your health and ease your anxiety especially if you are disciplined about it.

Thinking about the unknown and other future events that can go wrong serve as some sort of trigger points for anxiety. The aspects of yoga that deal with mindfulness and meditation help sufferers of anxiety, relieve the symptoms they feel. The way yoga works is that it changes the brain sensors by impacting on what is known as the GABA levels, resulting in the suppression of neural activity.

By being grateful for the opportunity to practice yoga, it is possible to notice a significant improvement in the life of the sufferer. Yoga has increasingly become popular over the years with many health and medical professionals also keying into the trend. It is even getting a lot easier to start a practice which has allowed a lot of centers to open up in virtually every city and town teaching and practicing different types of yoga depending on your level of proficiency. There are also a lot of YouTube channels that provide free resources in the practicing and studying of yoga.

However, before making any significant change in the type of exercises you want to involve yourself with or alter your diet, it is always better to consult your physician.

Practice Deep Breathing Techniques for Relieving Anxiety

By deliberately taking in slow and even amount of oxygen through a process of deep breaths can help restore a person who has already begun to show symptoms of anxiety and becoming dizzy, lightheaded or in a panic.

The practice of conscious breathing, while cultivating the thoughts of gratitude is one of the most effective known ways of managing and suppressing anxiety. Fortunately, there are no restrictions as to where you can practice it as it can be done anywhere.

This technique helps to slow down the heart rate leading to a reduction in the person's response to anxiety physiologically. It is considered a very excellent way of calming down the anxiety in a sufferer without involving the use of drugs or alcohol.

Toning the Vagus Nerve

A life of kindness and gratitude is one way of getting Vagus nerve toned. Depending on how well toned our Vagus nerve is will determine to a large extent how we adapt to stress and anxiety, it determines how well and quickly the body can recover to its state of equilibrium after a stressful or frightening event.

The Vagus nerve is the body's longest cranial nerve, it starts from somewhere around the base of the brain and runs all the way down to the middle part of the body. In doing so, it passes through the neck via the vocal cords, passes near the digestive system, spleen, heart, lungs, pancreas, and spleen. The Vagus nerve is a very important part of a person's parasympathetic nervous system and is the part of the nervous system that is responsible for how we rest and our body's capacity for managing digestion. The parasympathetic nervous system serves as a soothing and calming force in the body, which is different from the sympathetic nervous system primarily concerned with our "fight or flight" response to unwanted events.

Some of the ways of toning the Vagal nerve include practicing humming breathing, ujjayi breathing, singing, talking, chanting, showing kindness, and washing your face with ice or cold water, as commonplace and easy as these activities may be, high Vagal tone is able to improve how a large number of the body's system function and can lead to the reduction of heart attacks, strokes and even help in the regulation of the sugar levels in the blood. When next you come across someone who seems almost always contented and calm, chances are that the person has high levels of Vagal tone, low Vagal tone, on the other hand, is what increases the chances of having cardiovascular diseases, diabetes, fatigue, auto-immune disorder, stroke, Crohn and other forms of diseases which makes toning the Vagus Nerve so beneficial in treating anxiety naturally.

Lifestyle Management

As with other forms of physical and mental health-related issues, it always good to maintain and sustain a healthy lifestyle, eating and drinking healthy contents that have high nutritional values and low toxin levels. Eating healthy foods that have a healthy dose of carbohydrate, vitamins and other essential minerals play a great role in keeping you free from anxiety.

Taking less of high sugar diets, processed foods, an artificial preservative, and other chemicals while taking instead lean proteins, fruits, vegetables will go a long way in ensuring anxiety is brought down. Sufferers of anxiety should also make efforts to eliminate the amount of caffeine in their system because of its propensity to cause nervousness and make some people jittery.

A lot of people who suffer from anxiety, stress or depression tend to turn to alcohol and drug abuse to try and block their sensitivity to the issue as a short term measure, but the fact is that such measures only serve to aggravate the problem of anxiety disorder. These items tend to contain components that are not helpful in any way and are similar to smoking, which also serves as another form of quick-fix but with a tendency to worsen the anxiety over time.

Insomnia is both an effect and a cause of anxiety. Only by sleeping properly at night can a person be relieved from the stress associated with anxiety. Keeping your room cool and dark helps the body to sleep better and it creates an effect on the person's mood that helps maintain a balanced in the brain allowing it to rest properly and suppress depression and anxiety. Because people who do not get enough sleep at night both in terms of length and quality are more likely to develop symptoms of anxiety, depression, and stress compared to those who get enough night's sleep, it is important to try an aim for a sleep time of up to get 7-9 hours of sleep each night to be able to reduce stress, improve on balancing the body's hormones, combat moodiness and reduce fatigue. A diffusion of lavender or Roman chamomile essential oil into the body can also help to induce relaxation.

Also, as part of living a healthy lifestyle is the need to create time to play, laugh and smile. It also involves incorporating visiting fun places and open-air parks. You can also involve in hobbies like games, sports, painting, hiking, swimming, and dancing, and anything that can make you laugh and have fun. Use the opportunity to be free with people and let go of your emotions, hug as many people you can comfortably hug and bond with your loved ones, spouses, and kids. Your loved ones are going to feel safe, secure and a sense of affection.

Have a Strong Social Support System

Building a strong relationship and good social network is a very effective way of reducing isolations, being lonely and depressed. Being in the company of real friends, we can exchange banters with, and family members, we are comfortable with does a great job of helping to deal with anxiety and serving an unofficial therapeutic session and allows others notice the early signs of threats and sometimes offer a suggestion on what may have previously worked for them.

Another way of achieving having physical contact people is to join a class or group of people who have similar interest as you. People who have a similar purpose to us or who are better than us are also able to provide us the required support in handling the events of life. Similar to regular contacts with friends and family is the physical bonding with pets, studies show that caring for pets has an overall positive effect on us.

Conclusion

If you suffer from anxiety, it is difficult to imagine that gratitude can be a form of cure for anxiety, a lot of studies, however, support the fact that showing gratitude is a very effective way of dealing with anxiety. While trying to escape from anxiety, it is very important not to fall into the trap of substance abuse as a quick fix. The temporary relief provided by these substances (such as marijuana) and alcohol will be unproductive in the long run.

A more holistic approach tends to involve natural remedies that are psychological and physical in nature, which has been scientifically proven to be effective in lowering anxiety.

A lot of people find anxiety to be an inconveniencing condition that's associated with a general decline in overall physical, mental health and long-term stress. Because of how serious it can be, many people are unable to rationalize how it is possible for simple acts of gratitude can help to upturn the effects of anxiety.

As a matter of fact, it was not until a few years ago that the link between gratitude and anxiety began to be widespread until some ancient traditions have already known and harnessed the power of gratitude in relieving and treating anxiety.

Although this book was primarily about the use of gratitude in the management and relieving of the symptoms of anxiety, it can also be applied to a lot of other chronic diseases that you would expect only conventional medications to work. As you would have learned, combining gratitude with natural therapy and treatment for anxiety can become a lifestyle and offer a far more reaching solution to the treatment of anxiety.

Appendix

While in the process of expressing our gratitude, we must never lose sight of the fact that the highest level of appreciation or gratitude is not just by uttering words but by actually being thankful. For gratitude to be fully expressed in our lives, we must be ready to actively practice it in order for it to become a part of our daily life. In order to be fully inducted into the gratitude journey, you can adapt the use of a gratitude journal. This entails recording a daily activity on gratitude.

Below is a thirty-day action plan on gratitude that you can follow through to help you practice gratitude more which will ease anxiety in the long run:

Day 1

Think of five ways you can share your gratitude today and write them out.

- Say a thank you that you are alive
- Say a thank you to your colleagues for simple acts of kindness
- Say a thank you to your service providers like your steward
- Say thank to the security guard at your workplace
- Say thanks to your spouse for being there for you

Day 2

Identify your colleagues and those you work with, whom you have never said hello to or appreciated the things they do, especially those who are often ignored and looked down on.

Day 3

Express gratitude for the privilege to enjoy a meal and for the ability to differentiate between different dishes.

Day 4

Create an atmosphere where the people around you are able to express their gratitude to themselves especially among your loved ones.

Day 5

Be grateful for the days you are able to afford a meal and have a roof over your head.

Day 6

List out the list of items that you have and you cherish and be grateful for them, whatever they may be.

Day 7

Be grateful today for the country, state, city or town that you presently live in.

Day 8

Express gratitude for having a source of income or the source of income you wish to have.

Day 9

Show gratitude to your loved ones as it can be very easy to overlook them when it is time to show gratitude to them, even though they bear the brunt of our anger firsthand.

Day 10

Identify those activities you do now that you take for granted and would likely miss if you were to find yourself unable to do them and be grateful that you are presently able to do them.

Day 11

Appreciate anyone who has ever extended a hand of kindness towards you that you feel you have not appreciated well enough and use this opportunity to call them.

Day 12

Identify up to five parts of your body and be grateful for them. You can start with the physical parts of your body like your eyes, ears, nose, legs, hands that are obvious.

Day 13

Did you learn something new recently? You can express gratitude for it.

Day 14

Be grateful for the challenge you have experienced no matter how tough they may seem, appreciate the fact that situations could have been worse.

Day 15

Try to always be that person that is ready to say something nice to a frustrated colleague as a result of their workload.

Day 16

Identify anyone who may have had an influence on your life and write them a letter. Like your high school teacher for example.

Day 17

Express gratitude for the ability to be involved in your daily morning routine, for waking up each morning.

Day 18

Be grateful for your child's smile as they play around the home.

Day 19

Be thankful for the little progress that you are making in life, especially when you compare your present position to where you were previously.

Day 20

Appreciate the people who extended a hand of kindness to you this week.

Day 21

Express appreciation to your parents or guardians by calling them and sending a present to them.

Day 22

Today, take note of those people you are unable to get along with in spite of your best efforts and be grateful for the aspects of their lives you find positive, the positive energy from this exercise will increase the chances of you being able to get along with them.

Day 23

Identify up to five internal organs of your body and be grateful for them. Appreciate that without them, you could be in serious health condition.

Day 24

Express gratitude for the simple things you that you take for granted, even your laptop, alarm clock, your car, your dog, your friends.

Day 25

Show gratitude for the different natural elements of the earth.

Day 26

Extend your kindness to strangers you come across.

Day 27

Show gratitude for the music you enjoy and appreciate them.

Day 28

Be grateful for the natural talents you have and the skills you have acquired over time that has helped to advance your career.

Day 29

Be grateful for nontechnical skills like baking, swimming, cooking, driving, communication skills, sports, etc. They are often the ones needed to handle the primary needs of our life.

Day 30

Appreciate the messages that you have received from a loved one or a friend who reached out to you.

Here is One More Thing

If you enjoyed reading this book as much as I have enjoyed writing it, I'd appreciate if you can post a kind review in the comments section.

Your comment can go a long way in convincing someone who is yet to decide.

Your support means a lot to me.

If you want to suggest ways of improvement, you can contact me here.

Thanks once again for taking your time to read this book.

Portia